Fantastic Finishes

Great Last-Second, Come-from-Behind Victories

From the editors of SPORTS ILLUSTRATED FOR KIDS

FANTASTIC FINISHES
A SPORTS ILLUSTRATED FOR KIDS publication/July 1996

SPORTS ILLUSTRATEDFOR KIDS and are registered trademarks of Time Inc.

Cover and interior design: Pegi Goodman
Illustrations: Andy Levine

ISBN 1-886749-12-4

Fantastic Finishes is published by SPORTS ILLUSTRATED FOR KIDS, a division of Time Inc. Its trademark is registered in the U.S. Patent and Trademark Office and in other countries. SPORTS ILLUSTRATED FOR KIDS, 1271 Avenue of the Americas, New York, NY 10020

PRINTED IN THE UNITED STATES OF AMERICA

10 9 8 7 6 5 4 3 2 1

Front-cover photos: Bob Donnan (Michael Jordan); Walter Iooss Jr./Sports Illustrated (Dwight Clark); William R. Sallaz/Duomo (Oksana Baiul); Sports Illustrated (Kirby Puckett). **Back-cover photos:** John Hanlon/Sports Illustrated (John Elway); Reuters/Bettmann (Joe Carter)

Fantastic Finishes is a production of **SPORTS ILLUSTRATED FOR KIDS Books**: Cathrine Wolf, Editorial Director; Margaret Sieck, Senior Editor; Jill Safro, Stephen Thomas, Associate Editors; Sherie Holder, Assistant Editor

SPORTS ILLUSTRATED FOR KIDS Super Sports Book Club: David Gitow, Director; Peter Shapiro, Assistant Director; Mary Warner McGrade, Fulfillment Director; John Calvano, Editorial Operations Manager; Donna Miano-Ferrara, Production Manager; Allison Weiss, Associate Development Manager; Charlotte Siddiqui, Marketing Assistant

Contents

Ken Griffey, Junior
Page 28

Mary Lou Retton
Page 88

Bobby Hurley (left) scored big when Duke University met the University of Kentucky in one of the most exciting games in college basketball history. Read about the game on page 52.

Introduction

You have probably watched a game that came down to the last play or the final few seconds. Maybe you have even played in one! You know what it feels like: Your hands sweat, your heart races, you can't breathe. What's going to happen? Who is going to win? The suspense is *unbearable*.

It's also what makes playing or watching sports so much fun. Bottom-of-the-ninth home runs, sudden-death field goals, last-second baskets — these are the moments that make magical memories for sports fans and players alike. They create *Fantastic Finishes*.

This book is full of such moments. Flip through the pages and you'll find awesome endings of all kinds. There are outstanding plays, lucky breaks, great comebacks, and heartbreaking disappointments. Pick the ones that interest you or read them all. Either way, you'll experience the thrills and excitement that make sports great and make you a fan!

DIAMOND DRAMAS

Joe Delivers a Dream

If you have ever played baseball, you have probably had the following dream: It's the last game of the World Series. Your team is losing, and time to do anything about it is running out. Then, you step up to home plate and *POW!* You hit a home run to win the game *and* the Series! Your team instantly becomes the world champion — and you are the hero!

A lot of players dream of doing that. But in the long, long history of the World Series, no one had ever done it. No one had ever hit a home run to bring his team from behind and win the world championship. Until Joe Carter.

By 1993, Joe had played 11 seasons in the major leagues. He was one of baseball's most consistent power hitters. But the Toronto Blue Jay outfielder wasn't well known. He was not asked to play in many All-Star Games. He didn't have a snazzy nickname, and he wasn't flashy. He just did his job.

With Joe's help, the Blue Jays had won the World Series in 1992. In 1993, they were the best team in the American League (A.L.). They beat the Chicago White Sox in the A.L. championship series and then met the Philadelphia Phillies in the World Series.

The Blue Jays were a mix of experienced veterans and exciting young players. They were good, and they took the game very seriously. They didn't seem to smile a lot. The Phillies were a loosey-goosey bunch of guys who were fun to watch.

The Phillies had a left-handed relief pitcher named Mitch Williams. He had the nickname "Wild Thing," which described the way he looked *and* the way he behaved. He could be erratic. He would pitch well to one batter and terribly to the next. When he

Say What?

66 This is like, Do you believe in miracles? Yes, I do believe in miracles." — *Blue Jay slugger Joe Carter, after his Series-winning home run.*

66 I blew two games in the World Series. I feel terrible for letting my teammates down. But sulking doesn't bring the ball back over the fence." — *Phillie relief pitcher Mitch Williams.*

66 This happens in the backyard. Bottom of the ninth, down by one, and Joe pops one out of the park? You dream it all those years as a kid, and then here you are in the World Series and it happens?" — *Blue Jay pitcher Al Leiter.*

One swing of the bat turned Joe into a World Series hero.

came in with the Phillies leading, he sometimes walked batters and gave up hits, so it looked as if the other team was going to come back. Then he might strike out a player and get the win!

But the Phillies were struggling in the World Series. The Blue Jays won three of the first four games, including Game 4 — the highest-scoring World Series game ever played. Game 4 was the longest nine-inning night game in major league history. It took four hours 14 minutes. The two teams used 11 pitchers and scored 29 runs!

The Phillies blew a 14–9 lead when the Jays scored six runs in the eighth inning. Wild Thing went in to pitch during that inning, but instead of stopping the rally, he gave up the last three runs. Toronto won, 15–14.

Philadelphia came back the next night to win, 2–0. The Blue Jays went home to Toronto needing one victory to win it all.

Toronto jumped to a 5–1 lead in Game 6. But Lenny Dykstra hit a three-run homer and Philadelphia went ahead, 6–5.

In the bottom of the ninth, the Phillies put Wild Thing in to pitch again. He made it exciting right away. He walked Rickey Henderson on four balls. One out later, he gave up a single to Paul Molitor. That moved Rickey to second base.

Now, Joe came to bat. Joe had imagined this moment all his life — a chance to win the World Series with a home run. When he was a kid, in Oklahoma City, Oklahoma, Joe would hang around his father's gas station and pretend he was playing for the St. Louis Cardinals.

Joe pretended he was at bat with the championship on the line. Then he would shoot a rubber band up toward the roof of the station. If it made it up to the roof, it was a game-winning home run. If it didn't . . .

Now, the moment was real. Mitch's first pitch to Joe was an outside fastball. Ball 1. Another outside fastball made it 2 balls. Then another fastball . . . for a strike: 2 and 1. Mitch's next pitch was a good slider, and it fooled Joe. He looked awful as he made an off-balance swing: 2 balls, 2 strikes.

Mitch threw a hard, inside fastball. Joe reacted quickly. The ball flew off his bat toward leftfield.

For a few moments, Joe couldn't see it because the stadium lights got in his eyes.

Then Joe saw the ball. It was flying over the fence in left-field! Rickey came running home from second base. Paul followed Rickey across the plate. Fireworks exploded as Joe made his way around the bases, jumping up and down all the way. Joe's home run gave the Blue Jays an 8–6 victory — and the World Series!

"Baseball is kind of a lucky game," Joe said later. "Williams could have got me out, or I could have hit into a double play and *he'd* be the hero. It doesn't make him less a player or me more because I got a hit."

Maybe, but it did make Joe famous. After all, how many players deliver a dream come true?

Blast From The Past

Joe Carter is the only person to hit a ninth-inning, come-from-behind homer to win a World Series. But Bill Mazeroski hit an awfully exciting homer for the Pittsburgh Pirates in 1960. Bill's homer is the only game-winning home run ever hit in the bottom of the ninth inning of the seventh game of the World Series.

The Pirates and New York Yankees each had won three games when they met at Pittsburgh's Forbes Field on October 13, for Game 7. The game was a seesaw of thrills. First, the Pirates went ahead, 4–0. Then the Yanks led, 7–4. In the eighth, the Pirates got a break when a ground ball took a bad hop and smacked Yankee short-stop Tony Kubek in the throat. It should have been a double play. Instead, both runners were safe and the Pirates went on to score five runs for a 9–7 lead. The Yankees came back in the top of the ninth and scored two runs. Tie game.

In the bottom of the ninth, Bill, the Pirate second baseman, was up first. He slammed pitcher Ralph Terry's second pitch over the ivy-covered wall in leftfield. *Home run!* "Maz" jumped for joy and danced around the bases. The Pirates and their fans mobbed him. Maz became forever known as the man who won the World Series.

Twelve Endless Innings

Pete Rose of the Cincinnati Reds stepped up to home plate late in Game 6 of the 1975 World Series. "This is some kind of game, isn't it?" he asked catcher Carlton Fisk of the Boston Red Sox. It sure was! The game had everything: great fielding plays, clutch hitting, a game-saving throw from leftfield to home, extra innings. It didn't end until after midnight, but no one had trouble staying awake.

The Reds led the Series, three games to two. Three of those games had been decided by one run! Game 6 was played at Boston's famous Fenway Park. The Reds were hoping to end the Series with a show of the power that had helped them win an amazing 108 games during the regular season.

The Red Sox jumped to a 3–0 in the first inning. The Reds scored three runs in the fifth inning to tie the game. Then *they* took a three-run lead. Red Sox fans began to get a sinking feeling.

Going . . . going . . . Carlton smashed Pat's pitch deep to left.

Over the years, they had suffered through many disappointments when good Boston teams hadn't come through. It looked as if the Sox would lose again.

In the bottom of the eighth inning, Boston got two runners on base. Up stepped pinch-hitter Bernie Carbo. Bernie had smashed a three-run homer earlier in the series. Could he do it again? Yes! Bernie slammed a shot into the centerfield stands and tied the game, 6–6. The Red Sox were alive.

They almost won the game in the ninth inning. With one out and the bases loaded, centerfielder Fred Lynn came to bat. He had

had a great season and was later named the American League's Rookie of the Year *and* Most Valuable Player. Plus, he had homered in the first inning. But this time, Fred hit a ball high into the air and Red leftfielder George Foster made an easy catch. The runner on third base, Denny Doyle, decided to try to score on the play. He tagged up and raced toward home. George made a perfect throw home and Denny was out! Extra innings.

In the 11th inning, Cincinnati's Ken Griffey (the father of today's Seattle Mariner superstar) singled. Joe Morgan smacked a ball toward the rightfield fence. It looked like a double or a triple. Ken would score easily on either. But Boston rightfielder Dwight Evans went all the way back to the fence and made a spectacular leaping catch. Then he turned and fired a rocket throw to first base. *Double play*. The game continued.

The Reds had two men on base in the 12th inning when slugger Cesar Geronimo came to the plate to bat. Cesar was having a good series. Could he end the endless game? Not this time. He struck out to end the inning.

Carlton Fisk was the first Boston batter in the bottom of the 12th. He watched pitcher Pat Darcy's first pitch go by him for ball one.

THAT WAS THE YEAR 1975

○ The University of California at Los Angeles (UCLA) won its 10th national college basketball championship in 12 years.

○ Gerald Ford was president of the U.S. Two attempts to assassinate (kill) him were made during the month of September. Both times, he escaped injury.

○ O.J. Simpson of the Buffalo Bills led the NFL in rushing.

○ Rock singer Bruce Springsteen released the album "Born to Run," which made him a major star. He also appeared on the cover of *Time* magazine.

Pat then tried to slip a sinkerball past Carlton. It didn't work. Carlton blasted the pitch toward leftfield. The ball was flying! It would definitely go over the fence. The question was, Would it be fair or foul?

Carlton stood a few feet down the first-base line and waved his arms toward fair territory. The ball *hit* the foul pole! Two inches farther to the left, and the ball would have been foul. Instead, it was a home run! Carlton leaped around the bases as fans and teammates poured onto the field.

It felt like the Red Sox had won the World Series. But they hadn't. The next night, the Sox and the Reds put on another great battle in the seventh and deciding game. Boston took an early lead. Then Cincinnati caught up. In the ninth inning, the Reds' Joe Morgan lifted a single into short centerfield. Fred Lynn raced in to get the ball, but he couldn't reach it. A run scored and the Reds won the game, and the championship.

Boston had lost again. But if any team ever deserved to be considered "co-champions," the 1975 Red Sox certainly did.

CLOSE-UP

Are the Boston Red Sox jinxed? Some people say there is a curse on the team that dates back to 1919. That was the year they sold a young pitcher named Babe Ruth to the New York Yankees. Babe had helped the Red Sox win their fourth and fifth World Series, in 1916 and 1918. They haven't won a World Series since!

Boston has had many good teams and even has won the American League pennant four times — in 1946, 1967, 1975, and 1986. But each time, the Sox lost the World Series — in the seventh game!

Meanwhile, after Babe joined the Yankees, he became the greatest slugger in baseball history. He also turned the Yankees into winners: The Bronx Bombers, as they became known, won the World Series four times and the A.L. pennant seven times in the next 12 years!

15

Greatest Series Ever?

Baseball fans love a debate. And one of their best-loved debates is over naming the greatest World Series ever played. The 1991 World Series between the Minnesota Twins and Atlanta Braves gave fans a lot to debate.

Five of the Series' seven games were decided by one run, four of them on the last play of the game. Three games, including the last two, went into extra innings. Close plays at home plate, controversial calls, a scoreless tie for nine innings — this Series had it all!

The Twins won Game 1 easily. Then the fun started. Minnesota had a 2–1 lead in the third inning of Game 2 when a controversial call by first-base umpire Drew Coble shut down the Braves. With two outs and a man on base, Atlanta's Ron Gant singled to left.

Twin leftfielder Dan Gladden threw to third base but his throw was off. Pitcher Kevin Tapani fielded the ball and fired the ball to first baseman Kent Hrbek. Ron, who

Kirby rejoiced after hitting "the biggest home run" of his life.

had rounded first base, hurried back to the bag.

"*Out!*" said the umpire. Ron was outraged. He said he was back in time but Kent had lifted his leg off the base. An instant replay seemed to prove Ron right, but the umpire stuck to his call. Instead of having two runners on and slugger David Justice at bat, the Braves were out. The Twins took a two-game lead.

Game 3 was a four-hour, 12-inning marathon that ended in an instant. With Atlanta's David Justice on second base, Mark Lemke hit a single. The Twin leftfielder's throw home bounced twice . . . and David came sliding in just ahead of the catcher's tag! *Braves 5, Twins 4.*

Game 4 also ended with a play at the plate. Once again, Mark was the hero. Mark tripled and then scored on a sacrifice fly — but barely. He made a good slide to beat the throw and avoid the tag. *Atlanta 3, Minnesota 2.*

The Braves' comeback continued with a 14–5 victory. Now, they needed only one more win. But Twins All-Star outfielder Kirby Puckett wouldn't let them have it.

In Game 6, Kirby almost single-handedly beat the Braves. First, he prevented two Atlanta runs with a leaping catch. Then he put Minnesota ahead with a sacrifice fly. Finally, in the 11th inning, he hit a dramatic home run. *Twins 4, Braves 3.* "That was the biggest home run I ever hit," said Kirby.

The Series was tied at three games each. In Game 7,

Stats & Stuff

In the 1991 World Series:
- A World Series record three games went into extra innings. It was the first time since 1924 that Game 7 went into extra innings.
- Game 3 took four hours four minutes to play. The two teams used a World Series record 42 players.
- No major league team had finished last in its division one season and won the pennant the next year — until both the Twins and Braves did it in 1991!

two brilliant pitchers faced off: John Smoltz, for the Braves, and Jack Morris, for the Twins.

The tension was unbearable as the two teams battled to a scoreless tie through nine innings. Batters were getting hits, but were not scoring. In the eighth inning, both teams loaded the bases — and failed to score.

In the bottom of the 10th inning, Minnesota's Dan Gladden doubled and went to third on a sacrifice bunt. Atlanta's outfielders moved in. By playing closer to the infield, they would have a better chance to throw home and keep Dan from scoring.

Pitcher Alejandro Peña walked two batters on purpose to load the bases. The tension mounted. Pinch-hitter Gene Larkin stepped up to the plate. He slapped Alejandro's first pitch to left — over the head of the outfielder, who had just moved way in toward the infield!

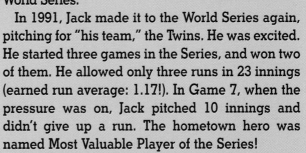

CLOSE-UP

Jack Morris grew up in St. Paul, Minnesota, rooting for the Twins. Then he went off and became an All-Star with the Tigers. He won more games than any other pitcher in the 1980's. He also helped the Tigers win the 1984 World Series.

In 1991, Jack made it to the World Series again, pitching for "his team," the Twins. He was excited. He started three games in the Series, and won two of them. He allowed only three runs in 23 innings (earned run average: 1.17!). In Game 7, when the pressure was on, Jack pitched 10 innings and didn't give up a run. The hometown hero was named Most Valuable Player of the Series!

After the game, Jack's sons Austin, age 10, and Erik, 8, ran onto the field to hug him. "What makes this so special is that they were here to see it," said Jack. "I hope they are proud of their daddy."

Dan scored. *Twins 1, Braves 0.*

"Someday down the road, people will look at this and they'll say, 'What a Series!' " said Twins pitcher Jack Morris. "I can't tell you whether it was the greatest, but I can tell you I'm proud to be a part of it."

A Really Sore Winner

It was the bottom of the ninth inning in the first game of the 1988 World Series, and the Los Angeles Dodgers were in trouble. They were losing, 4–3, to the Oakland A's. They had a man on first base, but they also had two outs. The A's had their nearly unhittable relief pitcher, Dennis Eckersley, on the mound and seemed one easy out away from victory.

In the dugout, Dodger manager Tommy Lasorda looked around for someone to save the day. Slugger Kirk Gibson stood in the corner of the dugout, bat in hand. He had been winning big games for the Dodgers with his clutch hitting all season. Could he do it again? Kirk nodded to the manager and headed toward home plate. The Dodger fans stood up and cheered. As Kirk slowly limped along, though, it was clear that what he needed was not fan support, but a new knee. His leg hurt so badly he could hardly walk. How could he hit?

The Dodgers had faith in Kirk. He had hit 25 home runs and driven in 76 runs that season. Cartoonists

Kirk could hardly walk, but his homer left the A's limping.

for the Los Angeles newspapers drew Kirk with a big *S* on his uniform. The *S* stood for "Superman."

Kirk *had* been super in the National League playoffs against the New York Mets, too. In Game 4, he hit a game-winning home run in the 12th inning. In Game 5, he crushed a monster three-run homer early in the game. He set up an important run in the ninth inning, when he singled and stole second base.

When Kirk stole second, he reinjured a muscle in his leg. All the Met fans in Shea Stadium cheered in admiration — and relief — as he was helped off the field. They were glad Kirk wouldn't be playing anymore that day!

Kirk was back for the next game and for the next. His leg hurt but he played as hard as he could. During the seventh game, Kirk hurt his knee badly sliding into second base. The Dodgers won the series, but they lost Kirk.

The Dodgers were big underdogs in the World Series. The A's were like an All-Star team. They had power hitters Jose Canseco and Mark McGwire and outstanding pitchers Dave Stewart and Dennis Eckersley.

Meanwhile, doctors said Kirk might not be able to play at all during the World Series because of his knee. No one gave the Dodgers much of a chance without Kirk in the lineup.

Jose Canseco got things going for the A's early in Game 1. In the second inning, he hit a grand-slam home run to give the A's a 4–2 lead. The Dodgers got a run back. They came to bat in the ninth inning with the score Oakland 4, Los Angeles 3.

Ace reliever Dennis Eckersley was on the mound, looking tough. Dennis was so hard to hit that the A's nearly always won when he came in to pitch. He got the first two Dodger batters out. Then, surprisingly, he walked pinch-hitter Mike Davis. Dennis rarely walked anyone. Pitcher Alejandro Peña was up next. The Dodgers needed another pinch-hitter. They needed Superman!

As Kirk limped toward the plate, he looked like anything but Superman. The Dodger fans screamed wildly. But they were a little worried, too: They knew that to hit with power, Kirk had to put weight on his injured knee. Kirk swung weakly at Dennis's first pitch and fouled it off: strike 1! Kirk fouled off the next pitch: strike 2! It looked as if Dennis was going to win this battle — and as if the A's would win the game.

But it wasn't over yet. Kirk's leg may have been a mess, but his eyes were still good. He fouled off a few more pitches and let three close ones go by for balls. The count was full: 3 balls and 2 strikes. The crowd yelled loudly as Dennis threw the next pitch. Kirk swung as hard as he could. *Crack!* The ball jumped off his bat and headed straight for the right-field seats. *Home run!* The Dodgers won, 5–4. Kirk could not even run around the bases. He did a combination of skipping and hopping — mostly using his good leg. He pumped his fist into the air and kept shouting.

That was only Game 1. The Dodgers needed to win three more games. No problem. They won three of the next four.

Kirk didn't play again. He didn't have to. The A's just couldn't bounce back from the shock of his homer.

The Dodgers, on the other hand, were inspired by it. Watching Kirk hit that homer when he could hardly stand up proved to the whole team that sometimes ordinary people do superhuman things.

Blast From The Past

Kirk Gibson's homer may have been the greatest in Dodger history. The *worst* was hit 37 years earlier, when the team played in Brooklyn, New York.

The date was October 3, 1951. The Dodgers were battling the New York Giants in the bottom of the ninth inning. The fierce local rivals had finished the season tied and were playing the last game of a three-game playoff to decide the National League champion. The Giants were losing, 4–2, but they had two runners on base with one out.

Bobby Thomson, the Giants' third baseman, stepped up to the plate. Dodger ace reliever Ralph Branca was pitching. He needed to get two outs and he knew it wouldn't be easy. Just two days before, Bobby had hit a homer off Ralph to win the first game, 3–1.

Now was Ralph's chance to get even. His first pitch to Bobby was called a strike. Ralph decided to throw the next pitch high and inside to tie Bobby up. But Bobby stepped back from the plate. He swung hard and connected. The ball flew like a rocket into the leftfield seats. *The Giants won the pennant!*

Bobby was an instant hero. Even U.S. soldiers fighting in Korea heard about his homer. It became known as "The Shot Heard 'Round the World."

23

Curses! Foiled Again

The Boston Red Sox were one strike away from winning the World Series. Players stood on the top step of the dugout. They were ready to run onto the field and celebrate. The Boston fans were beside themselves with excitement. They had been waiting for a baseball championship for many years. The Sox hadn't won one since 1918!

To make matters worse, the past three times the Red Sox had played in a World Series, they had battled all the way to the seventh game before losing. The Sox always seemed to break their fans' hearts.

At last, it looked as if the World Series trophy would be theirs! The Red Sox were leading the New York Mets, three games to two. It was the bottom of the 10th inning of Game 6, and Boston was ahead by two runs. Sox relief pitcher Calvin Schiraldi had two outs and two strikes on the Mets. It *had* to be over.

But the Mets were still alive, and that was dangerous. Earlier in the game, they had rallied from

24

Mookie's slow grounder didn't look much like a game-winner.

2–0 and 3–2 Boston leads. In the National League Championship Series the week before, they had staged several amazing comebacks to beat the Houston Astros. The Mets *never* gave up.

Met catcher Gary Carter limped up to the plate. He had been injured and was in a batting slump. But now he slapped a pitch into leftfield for a single. Then Rookie Kevin Mitchell punched a single right up the middle. There were men on first and second! Boston fans began to get nervous.

Met third baseman Ray Knight

was up next. Calvin got two quick strikes on him. One more strike and the Red Sox would be champs! Calvin wound up. He released the pitch . . . and Ray hit a single! A run scored. The Mets' tying run was on third base and the *winning* run was on first.

Red Sox fans were really worried now. They felt that Calvin had blown it. Boston manager John McNamara pulled him out of the game and put in reliever Bob Stanley. Maybe *he* could end this game!

The first batter Bob faced was Mookie Wilson. Again, the Red Sox got within one strike of winning the Series. With 2 balls and 2 strikes on Mookie, Bob fired a pitch toward home plate. The pitch was wild and it got past the catcher. While the catcher chased down the ball, Kevin Mitchell raced home with the tying run. Ray went to second base.

After two more fouls, Mookie hit a slow-rolling grounder toward first base. As the ball rolled toward first, it looked like an easy out for first baseman Bill Buckner. Bill was a tough player, but his legs were hurting. He hobbled over a few steps to make the play. It looked as if he had it, but wait . . . as Bill bent over, the ball went through his legs!

Ray Knight tore around third base and raced home with the winning run. The 1986 World

THAT WAS THE YEAR
1986

- Ronald Reagan was President of the United States.
- The space shuttle *Challenger* exploded. All seven crew members were killed.
- The Chicago Bears beat the New England Patriots, 46–10, in the Super Bowl. Defensive end Richard Dent was named the game's MVP.
- Halley's Comet swung closer to the Earth than anytime since 1910.
- Grant Hill celebrated his 14th birthday. Grant is now an NBA star.

Series was tied at three games each! Red Sox fans' long wait for a championship was going to have to wait.

Two days later, the Mets and Red Sox played Game 7. The Red Sox jumped to a quick 3–0 lead.

Then the Mets' magic took over. In the sixth inning, New York first baseman Keith Hernandez singled with the bases loaded. Gary Carter hit a single to drive in the tying run. The Red Sox had nothing left.

In the seventh inning, Ray Knight hit a home run to give the Mets the lead for good. The final score was New York 8, Boston 5. The New York Mets won the 1986 World Series.

And Red Sox fans went on waiting for a world championship.

Blast From The Past

The Mets aren't the only New York team that has crushed Red Sox dreams of a championship. In 1978, the Yankees ended the Red Sox' season with one of the most surprising comebacks in baseball history.

In July 1978, the Red Sox were leading the American League East division by 14 games. The Yankees were way behind, struggling to win and fighting among themselves. Then they got a new manager, Bob Lemon, and they started winning . . . and winning . . . . In September, the Yankees beat Boston four times, and the season ended with the teams tied.

A one-game playoff was held at Boston's Fenway Park on October 2. The Red Sox took a 2–0 lead. With one out in the top of the seventh inning, two Yankee batters hit singles.

One out later, shortstop Bucky Dent came to bat. Bucky had hit only four home runs all season. No one expected one from him now. *Surprise!* Bucky sent a pitch sailing toward leftfield. It hit the top of the wall for a *homer!* The Yankees led, 4–2.

In the ninth, two Boston stars had chances to save the season. Jim Rice slammed a pitch into deep right but it was caught. Carl Yastrzemski then hit a pop fly. It, too, was caught. The game ended — along with Boston's hope of a pennant.

Mariners' Ship Comes In

The Seattle Mariners had been a baseball shipwreck for almost 19 years. Between 1977 and 1995, they had only two winning seasons. Attendance at their home games was so low that the team was in danger of being moved to another city. Then, during eight surprising weeks in 1995, the Mariners finally got on a winning course.

The Mariners' magical voyage began on August 15, when they were 12 ½ games behind the first-place California Angels in the West division of the American League (A.L.). Seattle won an amazing 27 of their last 43 games and finished the season in a tie with the Angels. Then they won a special one-game playoff, 9–1, to win the division title!

Tired and happy, the Mariners flew to New York — and promptly lost the first two games of the best-of-five A.L. division playoff series against the Yankees. The second loss should have crushed Seattle's spirit. It lasted 5 hours 13 minutes, the longest post-season game ever.

Junior hit a record-setting five home runs against New York.

In the 12th inning, Ken Griffey, Junior, hit a homer to give Seattle a 5–4 lead, but the Yankees tied it right back up. The game went on.

It was 1:20 in the morning when Yankee catcher Jim Leyritz came to bat in the bottom of the 15th inning with a runner on base. He smashed a towering drive that cleared the rightfield fence. New York won, 7–5. Seattle was one loss from elimination.

"This team is not out of it," Junior said after the game. Mariner fans believed him. When the team returned to Seattle, they found signs everywhere that read REFUSE TO LOSE. There was even one on top of the 605-foot-high Space Needle tower!

The largest crowd (57,944) ever to attend a Mariner game showed up at the Kingdome for Game 3. Ace pitcher Randy Johnson blew the Yankees away with his 99-mile-per-hour fastball. He struck out 10 batters and Seattle won, 7–4.

The next evening, the Mariners again refused to lose. The Yankees led 5–0 in the third inning, but Seattle roared back to win, 11–8. Designated hitter Edgar Martinez drove in seven runs with a pair of homers. Junior hit his fourth home run of the series!

Game 5 was the showdown. It was full of gut-grinding tension. In the eighth inning, star pitcher David Cone was trying to protect the Yankees' 4–2 lead when Junior belted his *fifth* homer of the series.

Say What?

" These kids just don't quit. I think 'Refuse to Lose' is a great slogan." — *Seattle manager Lou Piniella, after the Mariners came back to beat the Yankees*

" That was fun. I always wanted to be in that situation where everyone is jumping on you." — *Mariner slugger Ken Griffey, Junior, after he scored the series-winning run*

" It's the greatest feeling in the world when you're on the other side, but it made me sick to my stomach." — *New York Yankee rightfielder Paul O'Neill*

Then, with two out, Seattle loaded the bases. David Cone pitched carefully to pinch-hitter Doug Strange. The count went to 3 balls and 2 strikes. David threw a forkball. Too low. Ball 4! David bent over and hung his head as the tying run was forced home.

The eighth inning ended without Seattle scoring again. Manager Lou Piniella decided to put in Randy Johnson. It was a gamble. Randy had had only one day of rest. He was tired, but he threw well until the 11th inning. Then New York scored a run on a walk, a sacrifice bunt, and a single. *Yankees 5, Mariners 4.* Could Seattle come back one more time?

In the bottom of the 11th, Seattle faced Jack McDowell. Jack had won 15 games that year, but he had never pitched in relief before. Joey Cora bunted and dove into first base safely ahead of the throw. Junior smacked a single. Edgar Martinez was up next.

Jack fired a high, inside pitch.

Stats & Stuff

In the 1995 A.L. divisional playoff:

◆ Edgar Martinez drove in seven runs in Game 4. That set a record for RBI's in one playoff game.

◆ Together, the Mariners and Yankees hit the most home runs (22) in one playoff series.

◆ When the series ended, the *Seattle Post-Intelligencer* newspaper printed the largest front-page headline it had run since World War II ended, in 1945. It read: "M's DO IT!"

Edgar lashed it into the leftfield corner. Joey scored as Junior flew around second base. Seattle third-base coach Sam Perlozzo wanted Junior to stop at third, but he was running too hard. The coach waved him home. The throw came to the plate. Junior slid . . . *Safe!*

The Kingdome was filled with a deafening roar. Junior was buried under a pile of joyous teammates. The Mariners won, 6–5.

For a long time after the game, the players stood on the field before the wildly cheering crowd. Baseball fans were no longer sleeping in Seattle. They were awake and in love with the Mariners.

The Drive

How can you tell whether a quarterback is really great? Watch him under pressure. Does he panic? Is he cool? Can he guide his team back to victory even when it's losing *big time*?

During his 16-year NFL career, in big game after big game, Joe Montana was Mr. Cool. Never was he cooler than during his first National Football Conference (NFC) championship game in 1982. Joe, age 25, was completing his first full year as the San Francisco 49ers' starting quarterback. The team had had an excellent season and hopes were high for the playoffs.

But beating Dallas wouldn't be easy: The Cowboys had won five NFC titles and played in five Super Bowls. The 49ers had never even won a league championship!

The game was like a roller-coaster ride. The 49ers jumped out to a 7-point lead. Then the Cowboys stomped back with a field goal and a touchdown. Joe threw another TD pass. *Again*, Dallas came back with a touchdown.

Dwight reached for the sky. He came down with a big win.

Early in the third quarter, the 49ers scored to take the lead for the third time. Then the Cowboys' defense began to get to Joe. He threw three interceptions and fumbled once. Dallas went ahead *again*, 27–21.

Time was running out on the 49ers. There was about five minutes left to play. The NFC championship was on the line. But victory was a touchdown — and 89 yards — away. That was when the 49ers began "The Drive."

San Francisco coach Bill Walsh and Joe tried to catch the Cowboys off guard by using more running plays. More important than the plays the 49ers chose to call was the way they performed those plays. Suddenly, everything started clicking. The 49ers marched steadily down the field. Joe tried a tricky play called a reverse. He started to his right, then handed off to receiver Freddie Solomon, who was heading in the opposite direction. He gained 14 yards! Joe passed to split end Dwight Clark for another 10 yards.

Only 90 seconds were left to play, and the 49ers were still 25 yards from the end zone. Joe calmly passed the ball to Freddie for a 12-yard gain.

On the next play, Joe missed a pass to Freddie that would have scored the winning touchdown. A running play gained seven yards and the 49ers had the

Stats & Stuff

◆ Two weeks after beating the Cowboys, the 49ers defeated the Cincinnati Bengals, 26–21, in the Super Bowl.

◆ The play that won the 1982 NFC championship is remembered simply as "the catch." But what about the throw?

"I wasn't going to take the sack," quarterback Joe Montana said after the game. "I couldn't see Dwight open. I knew he had to be there. I let the ball go."

◆ The 49ers' 1981 regular-season record of 13–3 was the best in the NFL.

◆ The Cowboys played in — and lost — the NFC championship in 1981, 1982, and 1983!

ball on the eight-yard line, with 58 seconds left. They were still 6 points behind. It was third down.

Joe didn't panic. The next play was a rollout pass. It was up to Joe to make the play work. He would have to take the ball and run to the right. He would look for a receiver in the end zone or run the ball himself.

Joe rolled out but he saw three Cowboy defenders chasing him. He raced toward the right sideline. Joe couldn't see him but he knew that Dwight Clark was supposed to be cutting across the back of the end zone. Joe fired an off-balance pass seconds before he was tackled. Dwight leaped high into the air, and caught the ball. *Touchdown!*

"The ball was over my head," Dwight said. "I thought, Oh-oh, I can't go that high. Something got me up there . . . God or something."

Blast From The Past

Joe Montana staged one of his first great comeback victories at the 1979 Cotton Bowl. The University of Houston was beating Notre Dame (Joe's team), 34–12, and Joe was sick. His body temperature had dropped to 96 degrees (down from the usual 98.6). Team doctors were trying to warm him up in the locker room. As soon as Joe's temperature approached normal, he bolted back onto the field.

In the next seven minutes, Joe completed seven of eight passes for 87 yards and two touchdowns. With six seconds left in the game, Notre Dame still trailed by 6 points and was eight yards from the end zone. Joe called a pass play, but his receiver fell down, so he "threw the ball away" (threw the ball to the ground, away from opposing players).

With two seconds to play, Joe tried the same play again. He faked the Houston defenders and then threw a great pass to receiver Kris Haines in the corner of the end zone.

The touchdown gave Notre Dame a 35–34 win!

Ray Wersching kicked the extra point to put San Francisco ahead, 28–27. With only 51 seconds left, the Cowboys couldn't score. The 49ers were headed to their first Super Bowl, thanks to Joe Cool.

Showdown in Miami

Every Thursday, the Boston College football team practiced the play they called "Flood Tip." It was a play B.C. rarely used. It was for the final moments of a game, when the Eagles were losing and had only one last chance to score. Here's how it works: Three wide receivers run down the field and end up in the same area of the end zone. The quarterback throws the ball far and high — in hopes that one of his receivers catches it before the opponents knock it down or intercept it. The play is a long shot, but in the final seconds, it could be B.C.'s only chance.

On November 23, 1984, the Eagles badly needed a long shot, last-chance play. They were losing, 45–41, to the University of Miami with just *six* seconds left to play. The ball was 48 yards from the end zone. How could the Eagles possibly win? Coach Jack Bicknell told quarterback Doug Flutie to try the Flood Tip.

The Miami–B.C. game had been billed as "The Battle of the Quarterbacks" because it featured two

With six seconds left, Doug fired the ball toward the end zone.

of the best quarterbacks in college football history. Boston's Doug Flutie was a small, quick, scrambling senior who always seemed to find a way to win. Bernie Kosar of Miami was a tall, curly haired sophomore who played as if he were much older.

Everyone watching the game in person or on TV knew the game would be a wild shoot-out because both quarterbacks were great passers. The only question was, Once the game ended and the smoke cleared, which one would walk away with the win?

The game lived up to all expectations. By halftime, the Eagles were winning 28–21. Forty-nine points, and it was only halftime! In the third quarter, Miami drove 96 yards for a touchdown, to tie the score. After field goals by both teams, the score was 31–31.

B.C. broke the tie with a field goal early in the fourth quarter. Then it was Miami's turn. Bernie handed the ball to running back Melvin Bratton at the Miami 48-yard line. Melvin ran all the way to the end zone. The touchdown put Miami ahead for the first time, 38–34.

But Doug had a reputation as a player who seemed to get better as the game came down to the wire. And he did. He led the Eagles on a another touchdown drive. Now B.C. was on top *again*, 41–38, with less than four minutes to play.

Bernie, too, stayed cool when games got close. Once more, he marched the Hurricanes down the field. He used up as much time as he could so that the Eagles wouldn't have time to do anything if they got the ball again. With 28 seconds left, Bernie gave the ball to Melvin again. Melvin scored his fourth touchdown of the day. *Miami 45, Boston College 41!*

After the kickoff, B.C. had the ball on its own 20-yard line. Several quick passes brought the ball to midfield. But there were only six seconds left! It was time to try the Flood Tip — the play the Eagles practiced every Thursday.

Doug took the snap and dropped back. A couple of big Miami defensive linemen rushed him hard. Doug scrambled away from them, looked downfield, and threw the ball hard into the wind and rain.

Despite all those practices, the B.C. players had not run the play correctly. Running back Steve

Strachan, for example, was supposed to stay in and block. Instead, he got excited and ran downfield.

Sometimes, though, you do not have to be perfect to succeed. Trying hard is often enough.

B.C. wide receiver Gerald Phelan had slipped between the Hurricane defensive backs near the goal line. At exactly the right moment, Gerald jumped as high as he could. The ball whistled through the outstretched arms of the Miami players and somehow ended up in Gerald's hands. He held on to it as he fell to the ground.

"When I rolled over," Gerald said later, "I could see writing on the ground. Colored writing. I was in the end zone!"

Yes, he was, and Boston College had won the game, 47–45.

Blast From The Past

The announcer could not believe his eyes. "Oh, my God, this is the most amazing, sensational, exciting, thrilling finish in the history of college football," he told audience. "I've never seen anything like it."

"It" was a wild, comical, mishmash of a play that will never be repeated. On November 20, 1982, Stanford University was beating the University of California (Cal), 20–19. Only a few seconds were left. To win, Cal would have to return the kickoff for a touchdown. But how?

A lateral pass is a pass that a player tosses to a player beside or behind him. Players are allowed to lateral after they have run with the ball. They are allowed to lateral almost anywhere, at anytime. And the Cal players did. Kevin Moen picked up the kick on the 44-yard line. He threw the ball to Richard Rodgers. Richard pitched it to Dwight Garner . . .

That's when the confusion started. Some players on the sidelines thought the game was over and ran onto the field. The Stanford marching band ran onto the field too!

The ball kept moving down the field, through the crowd. Finally, it ended up back in Kevin Moen's hands. He ran full speed through the band, cheerleaders, and extra players and into the end zone for a touchdown! Cal won, 25–20!

Buffalo Bounces Back

Pretend you are a fan of the Buffalo Bills. It's January 3, 1993. You are watching your team play the Houston Oilers in the 1993 AFC wild-card playoff game at Rich Stadium, in Buffalo, New York. The Bills are in big trouble. Star quarterback Jim Kelly can't play because of a knee injury. Top running back Thurman Thomas has hurt his hip and will miss most of the second half. All-Pro linebacker Cornelius Bennett is out with a leg injury. Ferocious defensive end Bruce Smith has three cracked ribs and is playing like a lamb. By halftime, the Bills are behind, 28–3.

Head coach Marv Levy is afraid his team is giving up. Coach Levy tells his players, "Whatever happens, you guys have to live with yourselves after today."

Early in the second half, Oiler safety Bubba McDowell intercepts a pass and runs 58 yards for a touchdown. Houston leads 35–3 with 28 minutes left to play in the

Nate's interception in overtime stopped the Oilers for good.

game. No NFL team has *ever* won after being behind 32 points so late in a game.

Okay, Bills fan, do you think your team can win this game? A number of Bills fans thought not and left. The Oilers thought the game was over, too.

But Bills backup quarterback Frank Reich *knew* that his team could still win. He just had to stay calm and be patient.

"One play at a time," Frank told himself as he took the field after Bubba's interception. Then he went out and led the Bills on the greatest comeback in NFL history! First, he drove the team 50 yards in 10 plays for a touchdown. *Houston 35, Buffalo 10*. Next, the Bills fooled the Oilers with an onside kick. The ball bounced crazily off an Oiler player and Buffalo recovered it at midfield. Four plays later, Frank fired a 38-yard touchdown pass to receiver Don Beebe. *Houston 35, Buffalo 17*.

"We're still up by 18 points," thought Oiler quarterback Warren Moon. "We're fine." Wrong! The Oilers couldn't move the ball and had to punt. The Bills took over on their own 41-yard line.

Four plays later, Frank threw another touchdown pass, to receiver Andre Reed. *Houston 35, Buffalo 24*.

Now Houston's defense was tired and shaken. Buffalo had scored three touchdowns in only 4½ minutes! The Bills were pumped. Buffalo linebacker Darryl Talley slapped teammates' backs and yelled, "Believe!"

Two plays later, Bills safety Henry Jones intercepted an Oiler pass. Again, Frank passed to Andre Reed for a touchdown. *Houston 35, Buffalo 31!*

The Bills had scored 28 points in the third quarter, and it still wasn't over!

The Oilers desperately tried to hang on to their lead. Warren led a long drive that was stopped at Buffalo's 14-yard line. On fourth down, the Oilers went for a field goal. But a big gust of wind blew the ball out of the hands of holder Greg Montgomery. Buffalo had the ball on the 26-yard line!

Frank went back to work. On third down, he surprised the Oilers with a running play. It gained 35 yards! Four plays later, Frank threw *another* touchdown pass to

Andre Reed. *Buffalo 38, Houston 35!* The Bills had the lead with only 3:08 left!

The crowd went bonkers, but the Oilers didn't quit. They drove downfield and kicked a 26-yard field goal with 12 seconds left. The game went to overtime.

The Oilers won the coin toss and chose to receive the first kickoff. Warren Moon completed two passes, then tried a third, to Ernest Givins. Ernest was knocked down by a Bills defender but no penalty was called. Buffalo cornerback Nate Odomes alertly grabbed the ball for an interception. The Bills had the ball!

A few moments later, Steve Christie kicked a 32-yard field goal. Final score: *Buffalo 41, Houston 38!*

Were you one of the Bills fans who left early? We hope not!

CLOSE-UP

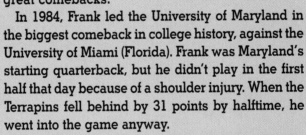

Buffalo quarterback Frank Reich spent 10 seasons as a backup with the Bills. He started only 12 games during that time, but he made the most of his opportunities. And Frank *knew* how to lead great comebacks.

In 1984, Frank led the University of Maryland in the biggest comeback in college history, against the University of Miami (Florida). Frank was Maryland's starting quarterback, but he didn't play in the first half that day because of a shoulder injury. When the Terrapins fell behind by 31 points by halftime, he went into the game anyway.

Frank calmly led Maryland on six touchdown drives in a row. He passed for three TDs, ran for one, and handed the ball off for the other two. The biggest play of the game came with about five minutes left in the game. Frank threw a pass that was tipped by a Miami defender. Maryland receiver Greg Hill grabbed the ball and ran 68 yards for a touchdown and a 35–34 Maryland lead. The final score was Maryland 42, Miami 40.

During the Bills' 1993 playoff game against the Oilers, Frank was reminded of that day. During halftime, a teammate told him, "You did it in college, you can do it here." And he did!

Franco's Miracle Catch

In 1972, fullback Franco Harris of the Pittsburgh Steelers had a great rookie season in the NFL. He rushed for more than 1,000 yards. He caught 21 passes and scored 11 touchdowns. Along with quarterback Terry Bradshaw and defensive lineman "Mean" Joe Greene, he helped turn the Steelers around. The team had its first winning season in nine years. Franco was named the AP's Offensive Rookie of the Year. But Franco's most amazing — and controversial — play of all came in the first round of the NFL's 1972 American Football Conference (AFC) playoffs.

The Steelers were playing the Oakland Raiders. Both teams had tough defenses, and no one scored in the first half. In the third quarter, though, the Steelers finally got on the scoreboard. They moved the football deep into Raider territory and kicked a field goal to take a 3–0 lead. Another field goal, with six minutes left in the game, gave the Steelers a 6–0 lead.

Because the Raiders were having trouble moving the ball, head

Franco ran 42 yards to turn his miracle catch into a touchdown.

coach John Madden had pulled his star quarterback, Daryle Lamonica, earlier the fourth quarter. He put in Ken Stabler.

Ken made Coach Madden look good. With the ball on the Steeler 30-yard line, Ken looked for a handoff, but no one was around. So, Ken decided to run the ball himself. He rolled left and ran untouched into the end zone for a touchdown! Kicker George Blanda made the extra point to give the Raiders a 7–6 lead.

There was only one minute 13 seconds left in the game. The Steelers scrambled to regain the lead. Pittsburgh quarterback Terry Bradshaw tried several pass plays. They moved the Steelers down the field some, but time was running out.

Only 22 seconds were left in the game now. The Steelers had the ball on their own 40-yard line. They *had* to score to win the game. Terry dropped back to pass. He spotted running back John "Frenchy" Fuqua at the Raiders' 35-yard line and fired the ball toward him. Frenchy was about to make the catch . . . then *whack!* Raider defensive back Jack Tatum slammed into Frenchy. The ball hit something or someone and went flying into the air.

It wasn't there for long. Franco Harris was just a few yards behind Frenchy and Jack — eyeing the loose ball. "When Terry Bradshaw put it in the air, I took off," Franco said. "I figured Frenchy might need a good block if he caught the ball."

But when the ball was knocked into the air, Franco went after it. He caught it at his shoelaces, scooping it up just a few inches off the ground! Then he streaked 42 yards into the end zone to score the winning touchdown.

The Pittsburgh fans and players started celebrating madly. But

THAT WAS THE YEAR
1972

- Swimmer Mark Spitz of the United States won seven gold medals in swimming at the Summer Olympics, in Munich, West Germany.
- Police caught five men breaking into the Democratic Party's national headquarters, in Washington, D.C. This incident started the Watergate scandal that forced President Richard Nixon to resign in 1974.
- Hank Aaron of the Atlanta Braves broke Babe Ruth's record for most home runs with one team. Hank hit his 660th homer against the Cincinnati Reds.

the Raiders were fuming. They said that Franco's touchdown should not count because, they thought, the ball had hit his teammate.

At the time, there was an NFL rule that said that an offensive player could not catch a pass that was tipped by a teammate. But it *was* legal to catch a pass that a defensive player from the *other* team had touched first.

The ball had hit something or someone before Franco caught it. Had it bounced off Frenchy, who played for the Steelers, or Raider Jack? The officials didn't agree with the Raiders. They ruled that the touchdown counted. Franco's "miracle catch" had won the game!

Franco and the Steelers had more great seasons ahead. Between 1975 and 1980, the Steelers won four Super Bowls. Franco became the Steelers' all-time rushing leader, with 11,950 yards. When he retired, after the 1984 season, he was the third-leading rusher in NFL history.

But nothing in Franco's great career topped that day in 1972 when his amazing catch "stole" an AFC championship for the Steelers.

CLOSE-UP

Pittsburgh Steeler owner Art Rooney was crushed. Oakland's backup quarterback, Ken Stabler, had just put the Raiders ahead, 7–6, in the first-round AFC playoff game against Art's Steelers.

With 22 seconds left to play and the Steelers a long way from the end zone, Art figured the game was over. He stood up in his owner's box in Pittsburgh's Three Rivers Stadium and headed to the locker room. He wanted to congratulate his players on their fine season and tell them he was sorry that they had lost.

A funny thing happened while Art was waiting for the elevator: Franco Harris made his miracle catch and scored a touchdown. The Steelers won, 13–7. Art missed it all.

But he did learn an important lesson: Don't leave your seat before the game is over!

98 Yards to Victory

The fans in Cleveland were crazy about their football team. Each Sunday, nearly 80,000 of them would pack into Cleveland Stadium and cheer frantically for their beloved Browns.

The kookiest of the fans sat in an area called the "Dawg Pound." The men and women in the Pound dressed up in dog masks, carried dog bones, and threw dog biscuits. They would yell so loud that players on the field couldn't hear one another. These fans were hungry for their team to get to the Super Bowl, a place the club had never, ever been.

On a cold January afternoon in 1987, the Browns looked as if they were finally going to change that. Cleveland was playing the Denver Broncos in the American Football Conference (AFC) Championship, and they were winning! The Browns were ahead, 20–13, with less than six minutes to play.

Things looked even better when the Broncos mishandled the Browns' kickoff. The Broncos

John left the Browns in the dust as he scrambled to victory.

ended up with the ball on their own two-yard line. Denver would have to move the ball 98 yards to score a touchdown. The Browns fans *knew* that wouldn't happen!

But the Broncos had John Elway. John was a strong, fast quarterback. No one in the league could throw the football harder than John. Few players had more confidence, either. As the Broncos gathered in the huddle, John smiled and promised them, "If you work hard, good things are going to happen."

That was easier said than done. The Browns' defense had shut down John and the Broncos all day. But this time, the Broncos were on the move. Steadily, almost easily, John carved up the Browns defense as if it weren't even there. Denver moved the ball 58 yards to the Cleveland 40-yard line.

But the Browns didn't give up. On first down, they pressed John so that he couldn't complete a pass. On second down, they sacked him back on the 49-yard line.

It was third down and 18 with less than two minutes left to play in the game. The Broncos *had* to move the ball at least 18 yards on the next play to get a first down. The Browns fans were screaming wildly. If their team could stop the Broncos here, they might go to the Super Bowl at last!

THAT WAS THE YEAR 1987

● On October 1, a major earthquake hit Southern California. It injured more than 100 people and killed six.

● First baseman Mark McGwire of the Oakland A's set a major league record for home runs by a rookie. He hit 49 homers in 151 games.

● The musical *Les Miserables* opened on Broadway.

● NBA legend Julius Erving retired after 16 seasons. "Dr. J," as he was known, scored 30,026 points and wowed fans with his high-flying dunks.

But the Browns couldn't stop John. He made a great 20-yard pass to wide receiver Mark Jackson. First down!

Now the ball was on the 28-yard line. Denver was heading into the Dawg Pound. The fans in the Dawg Pound were screaming, barking, and throwing bones.

That didn't bother John. He threw a 14-yard pass and ran for nine yards to move the ball to the five-yard line. Then, with just 39 seconds left, he threw a hard pass right into the belly of receiver Mark Jackson. *Touchdown!* John had driven the Broncos an astounding 98 yards in less than six minutes!

The extra point tied the game, 20–20, and it went to overtime. The Browns got the ball first, but couldn't get going. They punted.

When Denver got the ball, John kept up his great play. He threw one pass for 22 yards and another

CLOSE-UP

Denver quarterback John Elway has led the Broncos to so many come-from-behind wins (35 in 13 seasons) he could be called the Come-back Kid!

Rivals know that when John's playing, no lead is safe. "We shut him down the whole game," said one Cleveland defender after the '87 AFC Championship, "then in the last minutes, he showed what he was made of."

John is a great athlete. He played minor league baseball for the New York Yankees. At the same time, he was a football star at Stanford University. He quit baseball when the Broncos drafted him in 1983.

John holds an NFL record that may never be broken: He has passed for 3,000 yards and rushed for 200 yards in the same season seven straight years. No one else has done it five times in a row!

for 28. Denver ran a few running plays and then sent in kicker Rich Karlis to try for a 33-yard field goal. Rich's kick sailed between the goalposts for the victory.

The Broncos ran onto the field to celebrate. The broken-hearted Brown players and fans left, muttering about John Elway.

Good To The Last Shot

Some people say it was the greatest college basketball game ever played. That's a matter of opinion. These are the facts:

The game was the 1992 East Regional Final of the NCAA college basketball tournament. The 1991 defending champion Duke University played Kentucky. No one who saw the game will ever forget it.

After an amazing seesaw match through all four quarters of the regular game, and most of one overtime, Duke trailed Kentucky 103–102. There were only 2.1 seconds left on the clock. As soon as Duke threw the ball in and someone touched it, the clock would start. About as quickly as you could count one . . . two . . . the buzzer would sound and the game would be over. It was do-or-die time for the Duke Blue Devils.

Duke had been expected to win easily. They had a bigger, faster, and more experienced team. They were led by guard Bobby Hurley and center Christian Laettner.

With 2.1 seconds left in the game, Christian jumped and shot.

The Blue Devils also had a sophomore named Grant Hill coming off the bench. Duke was trying to become the first team in 19 years to win the NCAA tournament two years in a row. There was one problem: *No one told Kentucky.*

From the start of the game, each team went after the other with everything it had. Kentucky's defense threw Duke off its game. The Wildcats also shot well. They built an 8-point lead. But then Grant Hill came in and scored 5 quick points for Duke.

Duke led, 50–45, at the half, but then began to pull away. With 11:08 left in the game, Kentucky was trailing by 12 points. Coach Rick Pitino called a timeout. In the huddle, he told his team, "We have Duke right where we want them. Now we make our comeback." Duke coach Mike Krzyzewski

[sha-SHEF-ski] warned his players that Kentucky would not give up.

After the timeout, the Wildcats went wild. They scored 8 points in a minute and soon tied the score! The two teams traded baskets while the crowd roared. Finally, with the score tied, 93–93, Duke held the ball for a last shot. Bobby Hurley missed a running jumper with less than a second left. *Overtime!*

Duke and Kentucky continued to swap the lead in the overtime. Duke was ahead 102–101 with eight seconds left when Kentucky guard Sean Woods caught an inbound pass. He faked Bobby Hurley and launched a high, curving shot. The shot went just over the outstretched fingertips of Christian Laettner, who

Stats & Stuff

◆ Two years before the Kentucky game, Christian Laettner scored with less than a second left to beat Connecticut — and send Duke to the Final Four!

◆ The last team (before Duke) to win back-to-back NCAA titles was UCLA, in 1973. They won 10!

◆ The 1992 Blue Devils had four future NBA stars: Christian, Bobby Hurley, Grant Hill, and Antonio Lang.

was 6' 11" and jumping! The shot banked off the glass and right through the hoop!

The Wildcat players and fans went wild. They thought that would be the last shot of the game. But the Blue Devils quickly called timeout and the clock stopped with 2.1 seconds left. *Kentucky 103, Duke 102.*

Coach K's first words in the huddle were positive: "First of all, we're going to win, okay?" Then he told his team how to do it. To get the ball inbounds, Grant was to throw it to Christian, at the foul line. Christian would shoot or, if the pass was off, tip it to teammates cutting to the basket. The last time Duke had tried that play, Christian had caught the ball and stepped out-of-bounds. Duke lost that game.

When Grant got the ball, he saw Christian with two men guarding him. But the area above the foul line was empty, so that's where he aimed the pass. The ball flew 75

CLOSE-UP

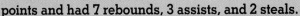

Christian Laettner had a perfect night against Kentucky. He made all 10 of the shots he took from the floor and all 10 of his free throws! Most important of all, of course, was the last-second jumper that won the game. He scored 31 points and had 7 rebounds, 3 assists, and 2 steals.

Christian was the first player ever to start in four Final Fours. He set NCAA tournament records for field goals attempted (167) and made (142). As a senior, he was named the College Player of the Year and was the only college player on the 1992 U.S. Olympic "Dream Team." Since 1992, Christian has played in the NBA, for the Minnesota Timeberwolves and the Atlanta Hawks.

feet — into Christian's hands. The clock started. Christian faked left, dribbled once, spun, and shot. The clock ran out, the buzzer went off — and the shot went in! *Final score: Duke 104, Kentucky 103.*

At the Final Four, Duke beat Indiana and Michigan to win its second straight NCAA title. But it was Christian's buzzer-beater that made it all possible.

A Wild Garden Party

Here's a riddle: What had three overtimes, two game-saving, last-second shots, one illegal timeout, one near fight, and a coach who collapsed from tension? The answer: the fifth game of the 1976 NBA championship finals — one of the most dramatic games in basketball history.

From 1946 until 1995, the Boston Celtics' home was the famous Boston Garden. Hundreds of NBA playoff games were played there, because the Celtics had many winning teams during those years. Of all those playoff games, though, the wildest was the one held on June 4, 1976.

The Celtics were playing the Phoenix Suns. The Celtics were considered the best team in the NBA's Eastern Conference.

The Suns had only the third-best regular-season record in the Western Conference. But they had upset the Seattle Super-Sonics and the Golden State Warriors to get to the finals.

Boston won the first two games

John (right) made two game-saving baskets for the Celtics.

of the series easily. Those games were played in the Boston Garden, where the Celtics rarely lost. Then, in Phoenix, the Suns won twice! Boston fans wondered what was going on. Few of them expected such tough play from the Suns. *No one* expected what happened in Game 5!

The game was played at Boston Garden. The Celtics jumped to a 36–18 lead in the first quarter and were ahead by 16 points at halftime. It looked as if the game would be a blowout.

Then, strange things began to happen. Suddenly, the Suns could not miss a shot and the Celtics couldn't make any! The Suns scored 11 straight points to tie the score, 68–68, in the third period.

With just 10 seconds left, Phoenix led by one point. Boston forward John Havlicek was fouled. John had won many games for the Celtics. If he made his two free throws now, he might win another one. But he made only one shot! *Phoenix 95, Boston 95.*

With three second left, John got the ball again. He sent a shot toward the basket, but it bounced off the rim as the buzzer sounded.

In overtime, John had the ball again with time running out. This time, he sank a basket — to tie the score and force *another* overtime.

With time running out in the second overtime, Phoenix had the lead and John had the ball *again*. He raced along the left side of the court and flung a running, one-handed shot toward the basket. It was good! That put Boston ahead by a point with one second left.

Celtic fans stormed onto the court to congratulate their heroes. But the game wasn't over! The referee signaled that two seconds remained. The fans thought the game should be over and attacked the ref. Police had to rush onto the court and arrest some fans.

Celtic coach Tom Heinsohn nearly collapsed from the tension. His assistant took over the team.

Phoenix had the ball under its own basket. How were the Suns going to get it all the way down the court in two seconds? Normally, they would call a timeout to get the ball at midcourt. But they had used all their timeouts. They couldn't call any more. Or could they?

They decided to call a timeout. The penalty for calling an illegal timeout was one free throw. Celtic Jo Jo White took the shot, and made it. Boston led by two points and the clock read 0:01.

Sun guard Garfield Heard received the inbounds pass. He turned and launched a high, arcing shot toward the basket.

The buzzer sounded. The ball dropped through the hoop! The score was tied, *again*. The teams had to play *another* overtime! No one could believe it. No NBA championship game had ever gone to three overtimes before.

The logjam finally broke in the third overtime. The Celtics led by 6 with 36 seconds remaining, and held on for a 128–126 victory. The game that wouldn't end was finally over!

Two nights later, Boston won the sixth game, 87–80, to end the Suns' season. The game was pretty tame compared to Game 5, but no one minded. One wild Garden party was enough!

Blast From The Past

John Havlicek had been saving games for the Celtics long before the 1976 series with the Suns.

In 1965, Boston met the Philadelphia 76ers in the Eastern Conference final. The series was a battle of big guys: 76er Wilt Chamberlain and Celtic Bill Russell. But John stole the show.

Five seconds were left to play in the decisive Game 7. The Celtics led by 1 point and had the ball under Philadelphia's basket. All they had to do was inbound the ball and hold on to it for five seconds.

Bill Russell had to get the ball inbounds. He saw Sam Jones breaking downcourt and threw a one-handed overhead pass toward him. But Bill's pass hit a wire holding up the 76er basket — and fell out-of-bounds! The Sixers got the ball.

Philly guard Hal Greer lobbed a pass to Chet Walker. Suddenly John Havlicek darted in front of the pass. He jumped as high as he could and tipped the ball to Sam Jones. Sam dribbled out the final seconds.

John stole the ball — and the show!

Giant Killers

For college basketball player Lorenzo Charles, everything seemed to be happening in slow motion. Lorenzo, a forward for North Carolina State University, was standing near his team's basket, while his teammates Dereck "Whitt" Whittenburg and Sidney Lowe dribbled out the remaining seconds of the game, Lorenzo waited for one of them to shoot the ball. He waited . . . and waited. Less than 10 seconds remained in the biggest game of Lorenzo's life.

He waited and watched the ball. Five seconds were left. Four seconds. Then, with three seconds remaining, Whitt let fly an impossible shot from what seemed like the edge of the universe. Lorenzo knew the ball wasn't going to reach the basket. He had to get to it — and *fast!*

The year was 1983. The place: Albuquerque, New Mexico. The event: The NCAA college basketball championship game. No one dreamed that Lorenzo Charles and

Lorenzo slam-dunked the ball — and Houston's hopes of winning.

his North Carolina State Wolfpack teammates would be playing in that game. Certainly no one believed the Wolfpack would be in a position to actually *win* the game. But there they were.

The Wolfpack had lost 10 games that season. They had to win the Atlantic Coast Conference (ACC) tournament to reach the NCAA tournament. To do that, N.C. State would have to beat two highly ranked teams: the University of North Carolina and the University of Virginia. Sure enough, N.C. State upset both teams!

In the national tournament, N.C. State had two close calls. It took two overtimes to beat Pepperdine University in the first round. Then, in the regional final, N.C. State faced Virginia again. The Wolfpack won *again*, 63–62.

N.C. State faced the University of Houston in the final. The Houston Cougars were a great team. Their players were so good at dunking that they were called the "Phi Slamma Jamma fraternity." Clyde "the Glide" Drexler and Akeem (now Hakeem) "the Dream" Olajuwon were the team's stars.

Most people thought the Wolfpack had *no* chance against the Cougars. They compared the game to the Bible story of David and Goliath. Houston was a giant compared to N.C. State.

The game turned out to be closer than many expected. But, in the second half, the Cougars went on a tear and outscored N.C. State, 17–2. Houston led, 52–45, and was in control.

Say What?

"I saw the shot was a little short. I was in the right place at the right time. I grabbed the ball and put it in." — *Forward Lorenzo Charles, on his game-winning dunk*

"The great thing about college basketball is that you win your national championship on the floor, not in some poll. . . .There's always hope. It's always too soon to quit." — *Coach Jim Valvano*

Then, for some reason, Houston coach Guy Lewis told his players to slow down the game. N.C. State scored 7 points in a row to tie the score at 52 with two minutes left in the game.

Wolfpack coach Jim Valvano told his players to foul a Cougar player who hadn't shot a foul shot all night. He missed the shot. N.C. State got the ball — and a chance to pull off the upset of the decade.

The final seconds ticked off the clock. Sidney Lowe tried to set up a final shot, but the ball was knocked away. Whitt recovered it, but he was 35 feet from the basket. There were only three seconds left! Whitt took a step forward and let the ball fly.

Everyone in the arena watched the ball as it arced through the air, toward the basket. Lorenzo realized the ball was going to fall short of the basket. He leaped into the air, grabbed it, and slammed it through the hoop — just as the final buzzer sounded!

For a few seconds, the crowd sat in stunned silence. Then Coach Valvano jumped high in the air and raced onto the court, hugging and kissing everyone he saw. *The Wolfpack had won the NCAA championship, 54–52!*

David had beaten Goliath again.

Stats & Stuff

◆ Houston was known for its terrific dunking ability. The Cougars had 11 slam dunks against the University of Louisville in the semi-final game. But in the championship game, they made only one dunk. The Wolfpack dunked twice!

◆ After the game, some people said that the University of Houston center should have been under the basket guarding Lorenzo Charles on the game-winning play. Who was that center? Akeem (now Hakeem) Olajuwon, who became a superstar with the NBA's Houston Rockets.

Actually, Akeem had a good game that night: He scored 20 points, had 18 rebounds, and was named the tournament's Most Outstanding Player.

◆ N.C. State was the first NCAA Championship team that had ever lost 10 games in a season. The Wolfpack's 1982–83 record was 26–10.

A Wild West Shoot-out

The 1970 National Basketball Association championship series was a wonderful matchup of two great, yet very different, teams: the Los Angeles Lakers and the New York Knicks. The series was as wonderful and exciting as you might expect. It went down to the last (the seventh) game and it had some amazingly dramatic moments. But for a fantastic finish, nothing could compare to Game 3.

By 1970, the Lakers were familiar with the Finals. They had played for the championship six times during the 1960's. Each time, they lost. It was frustrating, especially for Laker star Jerry West. Jerry was a great player. He had been in the league for 10 years and badly wanted to win an NBA championship and felt sure that 1970 was the Lakers' year.

Jerry was confident for two reasons: Wilt Chamberlain and Elgin Baylor. Wilt, a 7' center, was the greatest offensive player in bas-

Jerry (in yellow) drove hard in his quest of an NBA title

ketball history. He had been traded to the Lakers in 1968. Elgin, a forward, was an outstanding scorer and passer. Jerry was the best all-around guard in the league.

Wilt missed most of the 1969–70 season with an injury. When he returned for the playoffs, the "Big Three" played well together. They made the Lakers tough to beat.

The Knicks were younger and less experienced than L.A., but they played well together. They always passed the ball to the open man and helped one another out on defense.

The Knicks and Lakers each won a game to start the Final series. Then came Game 3. It was a battle of wills. First, it looked as if the Lakers would win . . . then the Knicks . . . then L.A. again . . .

The Lakers held a 14-point lead by halftime. Then the Knicks started hitting every shot they took. In the fourth quarter, they came within a point of the Lakers. But the Lakers stretched the lead back to 7 points.

The Knicks fought back *again,* tying the game, 96–96, with two minutes left in the game. Then Knick center Willis Reed hit a foul shot. New York was ahead for the first time all night!

The Lakers took the ball down the court, and Jerry West sank a jumper to put L.A. back in front with 38 seconds left. The Knicks' sweet-shooting guard Dick Barnett came right back with a shot from the corner. *Swish!* New York was ahead *again.*

The Lakers called a timeout to set up the next play. But before they could get it started, Dick fouled Wilt. Wilt was one of the worst free throw shooters in the league. During his career, he hit only about 50 percent of his free throws. (Most NBA players hit over 70 percent.) With the game on the line, Wilt missed the first foul shot. But he made the second. The game was tied *again.*

Only 13 seconds remained on the clock. The Knicks worked the ball inside. Forward Dave De-Busschere hit a short jumper to put them ahead, 102–100, with three seconds left.

The Lakers had used all their

THAT WAS THE YEAR
1970

- During a demonstration protesting the United States' invasion of Cambodia, four students were shot and killed by the National Guard, at Kent State University.
- NBA star Alonzo Mourning and tennis pro Gabriela Sabatini were born.
- The Baltimore Orioles beat the Cincinnati Reds in the World Series.
- *Rowan and Martin's Laugh-In* was the most popular show on TV.

timeouts. Wilt took the ball out-of-bounds under New York's basket and tossed it toward Jerry. Then, assuming the game was over, Wilt walked toward the locker room.

So, Wilt did not see Jerry dribble three steps and heave the ball toward the hoop from 10 feet behind midcourt. He did not see the 63-foot shot swish through the basket as the buzzer sounded. But he heard it!

The crowd roared! Wilt came back to the court in a hurry. In 1970, the NBA didn't have a 3-point line, so Jerry's shot was worth 2 points. That meant overtime!

In the overtime, the lead see-sawed again. But the Lakers couldn't pull off another fantastic finish. Willis Reed hit a foul shot to put New York ahead, 109–108, with 1:27 left. The final score was New York 111, Los Angeles 108.

CLOSE-UP

Willis Reed put the Knicks ahead for good in Game 3 with a free throw in overtime. But it was his performance in Game 7 that basketball fans remember best.

At 6' 8", Willis wasn't as big as some NBA centers, but he was as solid as a rock. He was the Knicks' captain and a major force for the team. After he hurt his thigh in Game 5, the Knicks lost, 135–113, in Game 6.

New York *needed* Willis for the final game. He received a shot for the pain in his leg and limped onto the court just before the tip-off. The crowd at New York's Madison Square Garden went wild.

After the tip-off, Willis hauled himself down the court and hit his first two shots. He didn't score again, but he didn't have to. His teammates were inspired by his attempt to play despite his pain, and raced to a 113–99 victory.

For Jerry West, the game was another bitter disappointment. He had played his heart out. He had scored 34 points, including the amazing 63-foot heave. The Lakers *still* lost.

Even the best from West could not beat the 1970 Knicks.

A Star Is Born

Sometimes, one moment will turn a good player into a superstar. Suddenly, everyone *knows* this athlete is special. Such a moment occurred on the night of March 29, 1982, when the University of North Carolina Tar Heels played the Georgetown University Hoyas in the NCAA championship game.

One of the largest crowds ever to see a college basketball game filled the Superdome, in New Orleans, Louisiana. Millions more people watched on TV as an 18-year-old freshman guard made a clutch, game-winning play that came to be known as "The Shot." The Shot made him a hero. It also gave the world its first look at the brilliant competitor who later became known as the greatest basketball player in history.

The young guard's name was Michael Jordan.

At the time, Michael was just another member of the Tar Heels. The team's best players were forward James Worthy and center Sam Perkins, two future NBA

Michael's shot beat Georgetown and propelled him to fame.

players. Michael had played well as a freshman: He scored an average of 13.5 points per game and was named the Atlantic Coast Conference Rookie of the Year. Still, his coaches never thought he would become a star.

There was a lot of pressure on the Tar Heels. They had the best record in college basketball that season (31–2). And they had not won a national championship since 1957. Now they faced the tough Hoyas, who were led by star center, Patrick Ewing.

The Tar Heels spent much of the first half trying to figure out how to score against Patrick. They got their first 8 points only when Patrick was called for defensive goaltending four times! (Patrick blocked the ball when it was falling into the Tar Heels' basket.) Still, thanks largely to James Worthy, they managed to keep the game close.

In the second half, the lead seesawed back and forth until the final minute. Georgetown was leading, 62–61, with 32 seconds left. Dean Smith, the Tar Heels' head coach, called a timeout. The team huddled around him as he planned the next play, perhaps the game-winning play.

THAT WAS THE YEAR 1982

- Some 20,000 soldiers from Israel invaded the Middle Eastern country of Lebanon to drive out Palestinian terrorists based there. Sadly, fighting in Lebanon was still going on in 1996.
- Wayne Gretzky of the Edmonton Oilers became the first NHL player to score more than 200 points in a season.
- *E.T.* was the most popular movie of the year.
- Cal Ripken, Junior, began his streak of consecutive games played. (He broke the major league record of 2,130 straight games in 1995.)
- The Oakland Raiders moved to Los Angeles.

The North Carolina players passed the ball around for a while. Jimmy Black faked a pass to Sam Perkins. Then Jimmy spotted Michael on the left side. There were 18 seconds left.

Michael caught Jimmy's pass and jumped into the air to shoot. He was 16 feet from the basket. Three Georgetown players closed in on him. Michael shot. The ball sailed toward the basket in a graceful arc and . . . *swish!* The Tar Heels were ahead, 63–62.

Georgetown still had a chance to win. With time running out, guard Sleepy Floyd got the ball and heaved it from midcourt. Everyone held his breath, but the shot missed as the buzzer sounded. The Tar Heels were the champions!

The victory meant a lot to Coach Smith. James Worthy was named the outstanding player of the tournament. But Michael became the biggest hero.

His hometown of Wilmington, North Carolina, held a Michael Jordan Day. A picture of him making The Shot appeared on the cover of the phone book. A restaurant near the university named a sandwich after him. Everywhere he went, Michael was mobbed by fans.

Fourteen years later, Michael is a nine-time NBA All-Star with the Chicago Bulls. He has done more amazing things in basketball than any other player in the history of the game. He is still being mobbed by fans.

But it all started with The Shot.

Say What?

"It all happened so fast that it seemed like we had won another game and that was it. I didn't know how much it meant to people." — *Michael Jordan, after his game-winning shot in the 1982 NCAA championship game*

"That kid has no idea of what he's done. He's a part of history, but he doesn't know it yet." — *Eddie Fogler, assistant coach of the University of North Carolina basketball team*

"I knew our lives would never be the same again. After that, we weren't private people anymore." — *James Jordan, Michael's dad*

Miracle on Ice

o you believe in miracles? In 1980, many Americans did. Why? Because they watched the U.S. hockey team beat the Soviet Union's hockey team. They did it at the biggest international sports event of all: the Olympics. Only a miracle could have made *that* happen!

Back then, the Soviet team was a hockey powerhouse. (The Soviet Union is no longer one country. In 1991, it broke into more than a dozen countries.) For practice, the Soviets would play All-Star teams from the NHL. They usually won. They had won gold medals in five of six Olympics.

To understand just how big this game was, you have to look at what else was happening in the world. In November 1979, Iranians had taken 52 Americans hostage at the U.S. Embassy in Teheran, Iran. The U.S. could not force Iran to let the people go. Also in 1979, the Soviet Union invaded the country of Afghanistan. The U.S. was angry about the invasion,

The U.S. hockey team went wild after its stunning upset.

but had been unable to do anything about it. To many people around the world, the U.S. didn't seem as strong and powerful as it used to it be.

Then along came the Olympic hockey team. Professionals were not allowed to compete in the Olympics. This team consisted mostly of college players who had played together for six months. They had more spirit than talent.

Most of the Soviet players had been together for eight years. Three days before the 1980 Games began, they crushed the U.S., 10–3. It didn't look good for the U.S.

In their first Olympic game, the Americans battled to a tie with Sweden. Then they upset Czechoslovakia and came from behind to beat Norway. The Americans advanced to the medal round. Their opponent: the Soviets!

The Soviets scored first, but Buzz Schneider tied it up for the U.S. The Soviets went ahead, 2–1. Winger Mark Johnson scored to tie the game *again*. After two periods, the Soviets were ahead once more.

Midway through the third period, Mark scored again to tie the game for the third time! The American fans couldn't believe it.

The U.S. players kept pressing. The pace of the game was frantic. Ninety seconds after Mark's second goal, U.S. captain Mike Eruzione

THAT WAS THE YEAR
1980

- Mike Schmidt led the Philadelphia Phillies to their first World Series title.
- Mount St. Helens woke up! The volcano, which is near Seattle, Washington, erupted for the first time since 1857.
- Camera buffs got a new toy this year. The hand-held video camera (also called a camcorder) was introduced by the Sony Corporation.
- Speed skater Eric Heiden of the U.S. set an amazing record. He became the first athlete to win five individual gold medals at the Winter Olympics!

[uh-ROO-zee-own-ee] took a slap shot from 30 feet out. Soviet goalie Vladimir Myshkin had no chance. *Score!* The U.S. was ahead for the first time all night!

The arena erupted. Thousands of people stood and cheered madly. They waved U.S. flags and chanted "U-S-A! U-S-A!"

The Soviets poured on the offense. But U.S. goalie Jim Craig turned away every shot for the last 10 minutes of the game. As the clock ticked down, the noise level went up even higher.

With 10 seconds to play, TV announcer Al Michaels stopped speaking. He let the TV viewers listen to the crowd. It counted down from 10 to 0. Then Al Michaels shouted, "Do you believe in miracles? *YES!*"

The Americans had beaten the mighty Soviets. Two days later, they beat Finland to win the gold medal! It was the first gold medal in hockey for the U.S. since 1960.

The whole country celebrated. The underdog college kids were Olympic champions.

Blast From The Past

Americans had high hopes for their 1960 Olympic hockey team. But the "Team of Destiny" was struggling. Just before the Games, the U.S. lost two games to college teams.

In the first Olympic game, the Americans trailed, 4–3, in the final period. Then, *boom!* Their luck changed. The U.S. fought back and won, 7–5.

After that, there was no stopping the Americans. They beat Australia, Sweden, Germany, and Canada. Then they faced the defending champion Soviet Union. The Soviets had never lost an Olympic hockey game to the United States . . . until that day. The U.S. won the game, 3–2!

The U.S. team played Czechoslovakia for the gold medal. After two sluggish periods, the Americans were behind, 4–3. Then came another scoring explosion. The U.S. scored six times in the third period and won, 9–4!

For the first time ever, the Americans were Olympic champions. They didn't repeat the feat for 20 years — until the "Miracle on Ice."

'El Rey' Reigns Supreme

Imagine you are playing in the World Cup of soccer. It's being held in Mexico, where soccer is king, and millions of soccer fans are watching, in person and on TV. You are from the South American country of Argentina, another hotbed of soccer. And remember, the World Cup is like the World Series, the Super Bowl, and the Final Four all rolled into one. Are you feeling a little nervous yet?

Now pretend that you are the best offensive player in the world. *Everyone* in Argentina is counting on you to help your national team win the World Cup. Everyone in the rest of the world knows how good you are — and is trying to stop you from winning.

If you can imagine all this, you have a good idea what it felt like to be in Diego Maradona's soccer cleats during the summer of 1986. Diego was only 25 years old, but he had the weight of the World Cup on his shoulders. How did Diego handle it? He was magnificent.

Argentina moved through the

The Germans were all over Diego (center), but he still won.

first round easily. In the quarter-finals, Argentina played England. Early in the second half, an English midfielder outbattled Diego for the ball and passed it back to his goalkeeper, Peter Shilton. Diego and Peter jumped for the ball at the same time. It ended up in the net. Many people said that Diego hit the ball with his hand, which is illegal. The referee said the goal counted.

Later, Diego took the ball more than 50 yards down the field by himself. He dodged English defenders with spectacular moves, and scored again. Argentina won, 2–1.

Before Argentina's semi-final game against Belgium, the Belgian goalie said, "Maradona is nothing special." Diego proved otherwise. He scored two goals. Argentina advanced to the championship game against West Germany. (At the time, Germany was divided into two countries, East and West.)

The West German team was tough and talented. Its coach, Franz Beckenbauer, knew Diego was great. "He is the best player in the World Cup, the best player in the world," he said. "We will do our best to put him out of the game, but it is almost impossible."

The West Germans surprised Argentina by attacking instead of depending on their solid defense. Only Argentina's excellent defense kept West Germany from scoring in the first half. West Germany guarded Diego closely — sometimes, too closely. Argentina scored on a free kick it received when a player fouled Diego.

In the second half, the great German player Karlheinz Foerster was given only one job: guard Diego. Instead of getting frustrated, Diego decided that he would find a way to get the ball to his teammates. Ten minutes into the second half, he did just that. Diego passed the ball to midfielder Hector Enrique, who passed to Jorge Valdano. Jorge scored! *Argentina 2, West Germany 0.*

Now, the pressure was on West Germany. Was Argentina going to run off with the Cup? In the second half, Coach Beckenbauer sent in Rudolf Voeller as a fresh attacker. With 17 minutes left in the game, Rudolf headed the ball to Karl-Heinz Rummenigge for a goal. On a corner kick seven minutes later, Rudolf scored to tie the game at 2–2!

Suddenly, the Argentina fans were worried. West Germany had come from behind to win the World Cup in both 1954 and 1974. Was history about to repeat itself?

Diego didn't think so. With six minutes left in the game, he got away from his defender and picked up a loose ball. He kicked a perfect pass through a line of *four* West German players. The pass went right to Jorge Burruchaga, who was running full speed to the West German goal. Jorge blasted a low, slanting shot past the diving goalkeeper into the back of the net! *Argentina 3, West Germany 2!*

The stadium exploded. West Germany had kept Maradona from scoring a single goal. But it had not kept him from winning the game, and the 1986 World Cup, for Argentina. Diego had lived up to his nickname, *El Rey* . . . the King.

Through Tears and Stitches

On Friday, February 25, 1994, Oksana Baiul woke up in pain. It was the day of the figure skating finals at the 1994 Winter Olympics. Oksana, a 16-year-old from Ukraine, had a chance to win the gold medal — *if* she could skate.

The day before, Oksana had crashed into another skater during practice. It was a scary, noisy crash. Oksana got a deep cut on her right shin and hurt her back. A doctor stitched the cut, but Oksana was very sore.

Oksana tried to practice on the morning of the finals, but she was in too much pain. She would need some medicine to ease the pain. Doctors received permission from the International Olympic Committee to give her a painkiller. They gave her two shots an hour before she competed. Still, she felt some pain as she went onto the ice.

Oksana was the 1993 world champion, but reporters at the Olympics had largely ignored her. They were too busy watching Americans Nancy Kerrigan, age

Oskana (above) edged out Nancy (right) to win the gold medal

24, and Tonya Harding, 23, the 1994 U.S. champion.

Nancy had won the bronze medal at the 1992 Olympics. But she was unable to compete at the 1994 U.S. Championships. She was attacked by a man, who hit her in the knee with a metal pipe. Nancy could not skate in the championships. She made the Olympic team anyway, but she had to work hard to get ready for the Games.

When police investigated, they found evidence that Tonya's husband, and maybe even Tonya herself, was involved in the attack!

At the Olympics, reporters followed Tonya and Nancy around to see if they would get into a fight. They forgot about Oksana — until the skating began.

Figure skating competitions have two parts. Nancy won the first part, the short program. Tonya placed 10th. She was out of it.

Oksana was in second place. She could beat Nancy if she won the long program (the second part of the competition). But then she had her crash. No one knew how that might affect the competition.

On the final night, Nancy performed her long program before Oksana. She skated well, but she made a few slight mistakes. Still, Nancy's scores were strong. They ranged from 5.7 to 5.9 (out of 6.0) for technical difficulty *and* for artistic impression.

Then it was Oksana's turn. She made some mistakes, too, but her program was harder than Nancy's. She put great feeling into the performance, and she skated with beauty and grace. Certainly, no one would have guessed that Oksana had been lying on the ice in pain the day before! Most of her scores were 5.8 or 5.9.

The judges then figured their "ordinals," which tell the order in which the judges think the skaters finished. Oksana won,

CLOSE-UP

Oksana had to overcome a lot more than physical pain to win the gold medal. She had to heal a broken heart.

When Oksana was a baby, her father and mother separated. Oksana's grandparents and her mom raised her. Then, Oksana's grandfather died. Then, her grandmother died, too. Worst of all, when Oksana was 13, her mother died of cancer.

Oksana had no home and no family. She was alone. After a while, she moved in with Galina Zmievskaya, a skating coach who had trained 1992 Olympic gold medalist Viktor Petrenko. Viktor helped support Oksana and, within two years, Oksana was the world and Olympic champion!

Oksana says that all the bad luck in her life made her strong for the Olympics. "This difficult life gave me the strength to compete," she says.

five votes to four. She was the Olympic champion!

When Oksana learned she had won, she cried, but her tears were tears of joy. Yes, her leg and back still hurt. But that pain faded when she felt the Olympic gold medal hanging from her neck.

King of the Court

The All-England Lawn Tennis Championships — known as Wimbledon because that is the name of the town where the tournament is played — is the most famous of the four tournaments that make up the Grand Slam (the other three are the Australian, French and U.S. Opens). Wimbledon is also the one players want to win the most.

During his great career, Bjorn [bee-YORN] Borg won 62 tournaments, including 11 Grand Slam singles titles. Bjorn was from Sweden. He had terrific ground strokes, so it was not surprising that he won the French Open six times. The French is played on clay, a surface that favors players with good ground strokes.

But it *was* surprising that Bjorn was able to win Wimbledon. Wimbledon is the only Grand Slam tournament played on grass. On grass, the ball skids and bounces much lower than it does on other surfaces. Wimbledon is usually won by players who "serve and

Bjorn (right) and John battled long and hard at Wimbledon.

volley," (serve and rush to the net to hit the ball *before* it bounces).

Early in his career, Bjorn lost in the early rounds at Wimbledon. So he worked hard to improve his serve and his volley. Before long, he started winning. In 1976, when he was just 20 years old, he won his first Wimbledon singles title. By the time he faced John McEnroe in the 1980 final, Bjorn had won four straight!

John, a New Yorker, was a great serve-and-volleyer. He was also well known for his bad manners on the court. In his semifinal match, John screamed at the umpire 14 times over one shot! No wonder the British fans booed loudly when he walked onto the court to play Bjorn in the final.

When the match began, John easily won the first set, 6–1. (That means he won six games and Bjorn won one.) But late in the second set, Bjorn hit two perfect backhand returns of John's serve to win the game and the set, 7–5. Bjorn was in gear.

Bjorn won the third set, 6–3. He was serving for the match with a 5–4 lead in the fourth. Bjorn had been serving so well that everyone thought the match was over. But John hit a few winners and won the game! Then, both men held serve and the score was 6–6. Time for a tiebreaker!

In a tiebreaker, the first player to reach 7 points wins. But, that player must win by 2 points — which means that a tiebreaker can go on for a long time. This one lasted 22 minutes! During the tiebreaker, Bjorn had 5 match points (chances to win the match by winning the point), but he didn't win any of them! John had 7 set points, but he was also having a hard time winning the key point. It seemed as if neither player was ever going to crack. On the 34th point

it finally happened: Bjorn cracked. John won the tiebreaker and the set, 18 points to 16. The match was tied again.

Like the rest of the match, the fifth set was *very* close. By the time Bjorn went ahead 6–5, he and John had played for almost four hours! John won the next game. Tie: 6–6. But at Wimbledon, the fifth set cannot be won by a tiebreaker; one player must win the fifth set by *two games*.

Bjorn served and won the 13th game and led, 7–6. In the next game, Bjorn was too good. He won the game, set, and match! He fell to his knees in joy and relief. Bjorn had won five Wimbledon singles titles in a row, a modern record. And he had done it by playing his best tennis.

Stats & Stuff

◆ Bjorn and John's tiebreaker was *not* the longest in Wimbledon history. In a first-round singles match in 1973, a 38-point tiebreaker was played, between Premjit Lall of India and . . . Bjorn Borg!

◆ "This is terrible. I'm going to lose." Bjorn Borg said to himself, after he lost the fourth set of the 1980 Wimbledon final.

◆ "He's won Wimbledon four straight times, he's just lost an 18–16 tiebreaker . . . . You'd think maybe just once he'd let up and say *forget it*. No. What he does out there . . ." John McEnroe, on Borg, after the final.

Seconds From Second

In 1989, Greg LeMond spent his summer bicycling through beautiful countryside. As he pedaled over lovely hills and majestic mountains and through green valleys and picturesque villages, though, Greg didn't pay much attention to the scenery. Instead, he pushed himself to ride as fast as he could. Greg was trying to win the most famous bike race in the world, and every single second counted.

The Tour de France is one of the toughest events in sports. Usually, it is longer than 2,000 miles and lasts for about 23 days. The Tour is divided into daily races called "stages." One day's stage might be a very difficult climb through the mountains. The next stage could take the racers through beautiful sunflower fields. At the end of the Tour, the rider with the lowest total time for all the stages is the winner.

After the first 22 days of the 1989 Tour, Greg had ridden more than 2,000 miles in a little over 87 hours. That meant he was bicycling about 23 miles per hour! Heading into the final stage, Greg was in second place, 50 seconds behind Laurent Fignon of France. That 50 seconds might as well have been 50 hours! There were only 15.2 miles left in the race, which meant that Greg had to ride about three seconds per mile faster than Laurent. *Highly* unlikely.

Still, Greg believed in himself. He had overcome bigger obstacles before. In 1986, Greg became the first American to win the Tour de France. Nine months later, he was nearly killed in a hunting accident. Not long after that, he had his appendix removed. *After that*, doctors operated to repair tendons in Greg's right leg.

A lot of people would have quit, but not Greg. More than anything,

he wanted to return to pro cycling. By 1989, he was back!

For most of the 1989 Tour, either Greg or Laurent Fignon led the race. After the fifth stage, Greg took the lead for the first time. He held it for five days. Then, during a stage in the mountains, Laurent passed Greg to go ahead.

Going into the last stage, a short time trial from Versailles to Paris, Laurent had his "gigantic" 50-second lead. (In a time trial, a cyclist rides as fast as he can by himself.) There were not too many people who thought Greg had a chance.

During the time trial, Greg never let up. At the midpoint, the timers checked their watches and blinked

Say What?

66 I showed him I was the strongest. If he wants the yellow jersey, he'll have to walk over my body." — *Laurent Fignon of France, after passing Greg LeMond to take the lead halfway through the 1989 Tour de France*

66 Unthinkable!" — *LeMond's former coach, Paul Koechli, on the possibility of Greg making up 50 seconds during the last stage of the race*

66 It's still possible." — *Greg LeMond, responding to the same question*

Greg roared into Paris and to his second Tour de France win.

hard. Greg was only 29 seconds behind Laurent! He was making up about three seconds per mile!

As Greg headed into the final stretch, he seemed to be flying. He was riding at nearly 34 miles per hour! But was it fast enough?

Soon after Greg crossed the finish line, Laurent came racing down the street. He was working as hard as he could, but it wasn't enough. Greg had won the 1989 Tour de France by just eight seconds! It was the closest finish in the 86-year history of the Tour.

In French, *LeMond* happens to mean "the world." At that moment in Paris, Greg LeMond was not only the best in the world, he was on top of the world!

Perfect Under Pressure

Mary Lou Retton knew something that her main rival, Ecaterina Szabo (*ZAH-bo*) of Romania, didn't. "I'm tougher than she is," Mary Lou told reporters before the all-around gymnastics competition at the 1984 Olympics. But would toughness be enough to help Mary Lou beat Ecaterina?

It certainly helped. In the finals of the competition, Mary Lou had to be at her very best in the last two events — and she was. Mary Lou did two perfect routines and won the gold medal by just 5/100ths of one point! Talk about tough.

Mary Lou, of Fairmont, West Virginia, had reason to believe she was tougher than Ecaterina. She had spent the last two years training with Bela Karolyi *[kah-ROLL-ee]*. Bela was one of the most demanding coaches in the world. Some gymnasts think Bela pushes too hard, but Mary Lou loved training with him.

Mary Lou had also overcome

Mary Lou's perfect vault landed her the gold medal!

setbacks on her way to the Games. Just weeks before the Olympics, Mary Lou had surgery on her knee. Doctors weren't sure she would be able to compete in the Olympics, but Mary Lou was determined to make it to the Games . . . and she did.

Entering the finals, Mary Lou led Ecaterina by just $^{15}/_{100}$ths of a point — 39.525 to 39.375. Mary Lou began the individual competition on the uneven parallel bars and balance beam, her weakest events. Ecaterina started on balance beam and floor exercise, her strongest. Here's how the evening went:

Rotation 1: Ecaterina did four back handsprings in a row on the balance beam and earned a perfect 10! Mary Lou's bar routine was shaky. She got a 9.85. The two were tied for first.

Rotation 2: Ecaterina was almost perfect in the floor routine and scored a 9.95. On the balance beam, Mary Lou wobbled when she tried a difficult back somersault. Her score was 9.8. Ecaterina now led by $^{15}/_{100}$ths of a point!

Rotation 3: In the vault, each gymnast does two vaults and keeps the higher score. On her first, Ecaterina earned a 9.9. Her second vault was worse, so she kept the 9.9.

Mary Lou was psyched. She knew her floor routine was more

THAT WAS THE YEAR

1984

- Geraldine Ferraro became the first woman to be nominated for vice president by a major political party. She and Democratic Party presidential candidate Walter Mondale lost the election to Ronald Reagan and George Bush.
- Pitcher Mike Witt of the California Angels pitched the tenth "perfect game" in major league baseball history. (In a perfect game, a pitcher doesn't let any opposing batter reach first base.)
- "The Cosby Show" was a big hit in its first season on television.

difficult than her competitors' routines — and she knew she could do it perfectly. She was right: The judges gave her a 10! Ecaterina led by only $5/100$ths of a point.

Rotation 4: Mary Lou was tough, but Ecaterina was no pushover. Under a lot of pressure, she did a beautiful routine on the bars. Mary Lou watched. "I knew it would be a 9.9," she said later. "I knew I had it."

While the judges debated Ecaterina's score, Mary Lou did her first vault. She did a complete flip and a double twist. She landed like an arrow hitting a bull's-eye. Mary Lou knew she had been perfect.

Before long, everyone else knew it, too. The judges gave her another 10! At almost the same time, Ecaterina's score was announced: It was 9.9. Mary Lou's perfect vault clinched the gold medal!

CLOSE-UP

Six weeks before the Olympics, it looked like Mary Lou might not even make it to the Games. She needed surgery on her left knee. Doctors weren't sure she could recover in time, but they didn't know Mary Lou! "Nobody was going to tell me what I could and couldn't do," Mary Lou said later.

Doctors operated on the knee using a tiny tool called an arthroscope. After arthroscopic surgery, most people need at least a couple weeks off before they resume sports. Mary Lou only took off two days! "I was a maniac," said Mary Lou. "I did three months of rehabilitation in about three weeks."

By the beginning of July, Mary Lou was practicing twice a day again. A few weeks later, she was in Los Angeles preparing for the Olympics. "I was completely ready," she said.

Although she didn't need to, Mary Lou decided to vault again. She received another 10! "Who could come back and do it again?" asked Coach Bela Karolyi later. "No other gymnast in the world could have done what Mary Lou did."

Talk about tough!

The Long Wait Ends

Fifty-four years. When the New York Rangers won the Stanley Cup in 1940, no one would have guessed that it would be another 54 years before they became NHL champions again. But it was. Fifty-four years is a very *long* time. To Ranger fans, the 54 years between National Hockey League championships seemed like forever. Although New York had many good teams over the years, they always seemed to lose the big games. And they often lost them in the most heartbreaking ways. Some people even thought the Rangers were cursed.

Fans of other teams would chant "1940!" to remind the Rangers and their fans of the last time they had won the Stanley Cup and how long it had been since. Finally, in 1994, the Rangers put an end to that cruel chant, but not before they made their fans sweat through two of the most heartstopping playoff games ever played.

The Rangers won their first two

Martin stopped Stephane's shot here, but not when it counted.

playoff series easily. Then they faced the New Jersey Devils in the Eastern Conference finals. After the Devils won three of the first five games, Ranger fans prepared for the worst. It didn't help any that Game 6 was to be played at New Jersey's home rink.

"We can win it and we're going to win it," Ranger center Mark Messier told reporters the day before the game. Mark's prediction made headlines, but he wasn't being cocky. He was trying to make his teammates confident.

Mark had played for five Stanley Cup championship teams as a member of the Edmonton Oilers from 1979 to 1991. His experience and leadership were big reasons why the Rangers had traded for him in 1991.

In Game 6, the Rangers quickly fell behind 2–0. In the third period, they were still losing 2–1. Mark's prediction didn't look too good. But then, Mark scored three goals and made good on his word. The Rangers won 4-2.

The seventh game was played at New York City's Madison Square Garden. The 18,200 fans who packed the arena howled "Let's Go Rangers!" from the start. The first period was full of tight defense and booming checks, but no goals.

About nine minutes into the second period, New York defenseman Brian Leetch rushed toward the Devils' goal. Brian fired a backhand shot that whistled between the skates of Devil goalie Martin Brodeur. *Score!*

The Rangers held their 1–0 lead into the third period. The Devils kept attacking, but Ranger goalie Mike Richter was sensational. When the arena announcer said, "Final minute!" the roar of the crowd sounded like a jumbo jet taking off!

Then New Jersey goalie Martin Brodeur skated to the bench so the Devils could send a sixth skater onto the ice. It was risky for the Devils to leave their goal undefended, but they *had* to score or their season was over.

To Ranger fans, the final minute seemed to last 54 years. Once, twice, three times, New York shot the puck out of their end. Each time, the puck was brought back to the Ranger end for a face-off.

Finally, there were only 18.6 seconds left. Mark lost a face-off and the puck went into the corner. Players from both teams fought for it. Suddenly, Devil right wing Claude Lemieux had it. He passed to left wing Valeri Zelepukin.

Valeri shot. *Save.* Rebound . . .

Valeri shot *again* . . .

In an instant, Madison Square Garden became as quiet as a church. Mark looked up at the ceiling in despair. Valeri had scored with only 7.7 seconds left.

Ranger fans feared the ghosts were coming back to haunt them. But Mark kept his teammates calm. He told them they had a great opportunity to prove their courage.